Amazing Autumn Baking Recipes

Heavenly Pastries to Bake Every Fall

by Olivia Rana

Olivia Rana © 2023

❁❁❁❁❁❁❁❁❁❁❁❁❁❁❁

License Notes

No part of this Book, either for personal use, commercial use, should be reproduced or distributed without full written permission from the author. This is prohibited by the law.

Also, this book is strictly meant to entertain you. As such, the reader is liable for any damages that the book or its content causes.

❀❀❀❀❀❀❀❀❀❀❀❀❀❀

Table of Contents

Introduction 6

    Additional Useful & Interesting Information 8

    1. Pumpkin Pie 9

    2. Maple Butterscotch Brownies 13

    3. Cranberry Bars 15

    4. Sweet Potato Pound Cake 17

    5. Apple Pecan Cake 20

    6. Pumpkin Brownies 23

    7. Pumpkin Bread 26

    8. Cinnamon Muffins 30

    9. Pumpkin Pecan Cheesecake 33

    10. Pumpkin Pecan Mini Pies 36

    11. Butter Pecan Cake 40

    12. Mixed Nut Bars 43

    13. Butter Pecan Cookie Bars 46

    14. Pecan Pumpkin Dessert 49

    15. Cinnamon Cookies 52

    16. Cranberry Banana Bread 55

    17. Pumpkin Muffins 58

    18. Oat & Coconut Cookies 61

19. Maple Cinnamon Rolls 64

20. Double Peanut Butter Cake 67

21. Cranberry Zucchini Cake 70

22. Spice Cake 73

23. Cinnamon Coffee Cake 77

24. Maple Butter Twist 80

25. Cookie Sticks 84

26. Butternut Squash Donuts 87

27. Cranberry Chip Cookies 90

28. Chocolate Chip Pumpkin Bread 93

29. Toffee Pear Pudding 95

30. Cranberry Drop Cookies 98

31. Sweet Potato Mini Cakes 101

32. Applesauce Spiced Cupcakes 104

33. Mexican Chocolate Pastries 107

34. Gingerbread Cake with Caramel 110

35. Spiced Pumpkin Bars 113

36. Caramel Apple Tart 115

37. Coffee Cookies 118

38. Dutch Apple Cake 121

39. Cashew Cookies 124

40. Pumpkin Cheesecake Dessert 127

41. Butter Brownies 130

42. Pumpkin Cookies 133

43. Cranberry Chip Cookies 136

44. Baked Apple Dumplings 139

45. Chocolate Maple Bars 141

46. Cranberry Muffins 144

47. Apple & Pear Coffee Cake 146

48. Sweet Potato Crisp 149

49. Pumpkin Chip Cookies 152

50. Gingerbread Scones 155

Conclusion 158

Biography 159

Afterword 160

Introduction

What is not to love about autumn?

Aside from the vibrant autumn colors you will find yourself surrounded with, it is just impossible to say no to amazingly delicious autumn pastries like pies, bars, pastries, cakes and many more.

During the season, you can enjoy the classic pumpkin pie or treat your family and friends to irresistible desserts like cranberry bars, butterscotch brownies, pear pudding, cinnamon rolls, sweet potato mini cakes and so on.

In this cookbook, you will find 50 autumn baking recipes that you will definitely enjoy making.

Each recipe is perfect for the season, not only using freshly available ingredients but also designed to be prepared with ease and convenience.

Whether you would like to make desserts for yourself to satiate your craving or enough to feed a crowd, you will find something practical from the recipe collection.

Additional Useful & Interesting Information

Here are some baking tips to help you achieve baking success:

- Follow the recommended butter consistency. If a recipe calls for softened butter, use softened butter. If it requires melted butter, then heat the butter first in a pan until melted before using. Butter consistency affects the texture of the pastry you are making.
- Read the recipe first before starting. Make sure that you read the recipe procedure carefully and prepare the ingredients first before you start. This helps you avoid baking disasters.
- Measure with care. All ingredients must be measured carefully. Baking is not like cooking in which you can adjust the quantity of ingredients. You need to follow the correct measurements to get the best results.
- Avoid ingredient substitutions. You can substitute the ingredients if the recipe allows it. Otherwise, make sure to follow the recipe ingredients to the dot.
- Keep the oven door closed during baking. It may be tempting to open the oven door to peek but resist the urge to do so. Opening the oven door can ruin the temperature and disrupt the proper baking process.

1. Pumpkin Pie

Nothing ushers in autumn like the classic pumpkin pie. Here is a recipe that lets you do the amazing dessert without extra fuss. Just do not forget the secret to making sure the crust does not get soggy; bake the pie on the lowest rack inside your oven.

Serving Size: 8

Preparation & Cooking Time: 1 hour and 10 minutes

Ingredients:

- 1 cup all-purpose flour
- 1 teaspoon white sugar
- ¼ teaspoon salt
- 3 tablespoons canola oil
- 1 tablespoon butter, melted
- 2 tablespoons cold water

Filling

- 1 egg
- 1 egg white
- ¼ cup white sugar
- ½ cup brown sugar
- ½ teaspoon ground cinnamon
- ½ teaspoon salt
- 1/8 teaspoon ground cloves
- 1/8 teaspoon ground nutmeg
- 1/8 teaspoon ground allspice
- 15 oz. canned pumpkin puree
- 1 cup nonfat evaporated milk

Instructions:

Add the all-purpose flour, white sugar and salt to a bowl.

Stir until fully combined.

Pour in the canola oil and butter.

Mix until crumbly.

Stir in the cold water.

Roll out the crust into a circle.

Freeze for 10 to 12 minutes.

Add the crust to a pie plate.

Trim and flute the edges.

Refrigerate for 10 minutes.

Use a leaf cookie cutter to cut leaves from the leftover dough.

Add the leaves to a baking pan.

Bake the leaves at 375 degrees F for 5 minutes.

Let cool on a wire rack.

In a bowl, beat together the egg, egg white, white sugar, brown sugar, ground cinnamon, ground nutmeg, ground cloves, ground allspice and salt.

Mix well.

Stir in the canned pumpkin puree and nonfat evaporated milk.

Pour the mixture over the crust.

Bake at 375 degrees F for 45 minutes.

Let cool on a wire rack.

Garnish with the leaves before serving.

2. Maple Butterscotch Brownies

You will relish every delicious bite of these brownies. The amazing treat is sweet, chewy and tender all at the same time. Serve it for family and friends to enjoy.

Serving Size: 16

Preparation & Cooking Time: 45 minutes

Ingredients:

- 1 teaspoon baking powder
- 1 ½ cups all-purpose flour
- ½ cup butter, melted
- 1 ¼ cups brown sugar
- 1 ½ teaspoons maple flavoring
- 2 eggs
- 1 cup walnuts, chopped

Instructions:

Preheat your oven to 350 degrees F.

In a bowl, combine the all-purpose flour and baking powder.

In another bowl, mix the butter, brown sugar and maple flavoring.

Beat in the eggs.

Add the flour mixture to the butter mixture.

Mix well.

Fold in the walnuts.

Spread the mixture into a baking pan.

Bake in the oven for 30 to 35 minutes.

Let cool on a wire rack before slicing into bars.

3. Cranberry Bars

It would be a great idea to make a big batch of these bars as they will usually be gone before you know it. Do not be surprised when you bring them to a party and you come back with an empty baking pan. For an extra special touch, serve them with orange curd, whipped cream or caramel sauce.

Serving Size: 20

Preparation & Cooking Time: 1 hour and 10 minutes

Ingredients:

- 3 eggs
- 2 cups brown sugar
- ¾ cup butter
- 1 teaspoon almond extract
- 2 cups all-purpose flour
- 2/3 cup pecans, chopped
- 2 ½ cups cranberries

Instructions:

Preheat your oven to 350 degrees F.

Whisk together the eggs and brown sugar in a bowl.

Stir in the butter and almond extract.

Gradually add the all-purpose flour to the mixture.

Mix until fully combined.

Fold in the pecans and cranberries.

Spread the mixture into a baking pan.

Bake in the oven for 45 to 50 minutes.

4. Sweet Potato Pound Cake

This pound cake comes beautifully out of the oven. Top with orange glaze before serving. Everyone will find it hard to resist!

Serving Size: 16

Preparation & Cooking Time: 1 hour and 20 minutes

Ingredients:

- Butter
- Flour
- 2 cups sugar
- 1 cup butter, softened
- 4 eggs
- ½ teaspoon baking soda
- 2 teaspoons baking powder
- 3 cups all-purpose flour
- ¼ teaspoon ground nutmeg
- 1 teaspoon ground cinnamon
- 1 teaspoon vanilla extract
- ¼ teaspoon salt
- 2 cups sweet potatoes, cooked and mashed

Glaze

- 4 teaspoons orange juice
- 1 teaspoon orange zest
- 1 cup confectioners' sugar

Instructions:

Preheat your oven to 350 degrees F.

Grease a fluted tube pan with butter and dust it with flour.

Beat together the sugar and butter until fluffy.

Stir in the eggs and vanilla extract.

In another bowl, combine the all-purpose flour, baking powder, baking soda, ground cinnamon, ground nutmeg and salt.

Add the flour mixture to the butter mixture.

Fold in the sweet potatoes.

Mix well.

Transfer the mixture to the tube pan.

Bake in the oven for 50 minutes.

Let cool on a wire rack for 10 minutes.

In a bowl, mix the orange juice, orange zest and confectioners' sugar.

Drizzle the glaze over the cake before serving.

5. Apple Pecan Cake

This cake deserves all the attention it gets. Not only does the recipe give you an incredibly luscious treat, but it is also very easy to prepare. This is indeed the perfect way to celebrate the autumn season.

Serving Size: 20

Preparation & Cooking Time: 1 hour and 20 minutes

Ingredients:

- Butter
- 1 cup brown sugar
- ½ cup butter, softened
- 3 eggs
- 2 cups unsweetened applesauce
- 2 tablespoons orange juice
- 3 cups all-purpose flour
- ½ teaspoon baking soda
- ¾ teaspoon ground allspice
- ¼ teaspoon ground nutmeg
- 1 teaspoon ground cinnamon
- 1 teaspoon salt
- 1 cup pecans, chopped
- 3 cups apple, peeled and chopped
- Hot caramel ice cream topping

Instructions:

Preheat your oven to 350 degrees F.

Grease your baking pan with butter.

In a bowl, mix the brown sugar and butter.

Stir in the eggs, unsweetened applesauce and orange juice.

In another bowl, combine the all-purpose flour, baking soda, ground nutmeg, ground allspice, ground cinnamon and salt.

Add the flour mixture to the butter mixture.

Fold in the pecans and apple.

Transfer the mixture to the baking pan.

Bake in the oven for 45 to 50 minutes.

Drizzle with hot caramel ice cream topping.

Let cool for 10 minutes before slicing and serving.

6. Pumpkin Brownies

These brownies will easily become your favorite. You will enjoy the delicious combination of chocolate and pumpkin. You can also add walnuts or chocolate chips to the batter before baking if you like.

Serving Size: 20

Preparation & Cooking Time: 50 minutes

Ingredients:

- Butter

Chocolate Batter

- ¾ cup all-purpose flour
- ½ teaspoon salt
- ¼ teaspoon baking soda
- 2 eggs
- ¼ cup cocoa powder
- 1 cup sugar
- ½ cup canola oil
- 1 teaspoon vanilla extract

Pumpkin Batter

- 1 cup all-purpose flour
- ¼ teaspoon baking soda
- ½ teaspoon pumpkin pie spice
- 1 cup sugar
- ½ teaspoon salt
- 2 eggs
- ¾ cup canned pumpkin puree

Instructions:

Preheat your oven to 350 degrees F.

Line your baking pan with parchment paper.

Grease the parchment paper with butter.

In a bowl, mix the all-purpose flour, baking soda, cocoa powder, sugar and salt.

Beat in the eggs, canola oil and vanilla extract.

In another bowl, combine the all-purpose flour, baking soda, pumpkin pie spice, sugar and salt.

Stir in the eggs and canned pumpkin puree.

Spread a layer of the chocolate batter in the baking pan.

Top with the pumpkin batter.

Swirl the mixture using a spatula.

Bake in the oven for 30 minutes.

Let cool on a wire rack for 15 minutes before slicing.

7. Pumpkin Bread

Pumpkin, walnuts, raisins and cream cheese come together to make this delicious bread that easily becomes a family tradition. It can be stored in the refrigerator for up to a week.

Serving Size: 24

Preparation & Cooking Time: 1 hour and 30 minutes

Ingredients:

Filling

- Butter
- Flour
- 16 oz. cream cheese, softened
- 1 egg
- ¼ cup milk
- ¼ cup brown sugar

Bread

- 4 eggs
- 3 cups sugar
- 45 oz. pumpkin puree
- 1 cup water
- 1 cup canola oil
- 1 teaspoon baking powder
- 2 teaspoons baking soda
- 4 cups all-purpose flour
- 4 teaspoons pumpkin pie spice
- ½ teaspoon ground cloves
- 1 ½ teaspoons ground cinnamon
- 1 teaspoon ground nutmeg
- 1 teaspoon salt
- 1 cup raisins
- ½ cup dates, chopped

- 1 cup walnuts, chopped

Topping

- 3 tablespoons milk
- 1 cup confectioners' sugar
- ¼ teaspoon vanilla extract
- Walnuts, chopped

Instructions:

Preheat your oven to 350 degrees F.

Grease 3 loaf pans with butter and dust them with flour.

In a bowl, mix the cream cheese, egg, milk and brown sugar.

In another bowl, combine the eggs, sugar, pumpkin puree, water and canola oil.

In a third bowl, add the all-purpose flour, baking powder, baking soda, pumpkin pie spice, ground cinnamon, ground cloves, ground nutmeg and salt.

Add the flour mixture to the pumpkin puree mixture.

Fold in the raisins, dates and walnuts.

Pour the batter into the 3 loaf pans.

Cut through the mixture and add the filling. Swirl with a knife.

Bake in the oven for 1 hour and 10 minutes.

Let cool for 10 minutes.

In a small bowl, mix the milk, confectioners' sugar and vanilla extract.

Drizzle the mixture over the bread and top it with walnuts.

8. Cinnamon Muffins

These muffins are a delightful treat that you would love to bring to potluck parties. You will get rave reviews each time. You can make a big batch and freeze for up to 3 months.

Serving Size: 12

Preparation & Cooking Time: 30 minutes

Ingredients:

- ½ cup sugar
- 1/3 cup shortening
- 1 egg
- 1 ½ cups all-purpose flour
- 1 ½ teaspoons baking powder
- ¼ teaspoon ground nutmeg
- 2 teaspoons ground cinnamon
- ½ teaspoon salt
- ½ cup milk

Topping

- 3 tablespoons butter, melted
- ½ cup sugar
- 1 ½ teaspoons ground cinnamon

Instructions:

Cream the sugar and shortening until fluffy.

Stir in the egg.

In another bowl, combine the baking powder, all-purpose flour, ground cinnamon, ground nutmeg and salt.

Add the flour mixture to the sugar mixture.

Pour in the milk.

Mix well.

Pour the mixture into muffin cups.

Bake in the oven at 350 degrees F for 20 minutes.

In a small bowl, mix the ground cinnamon and sugar.

Dip the muffins in the butter and sprinkle them with the cinnamon sugar.

9. Pumpkin Pecan Cheesecake

This pie impresses you to no end not only with its delicious flavor but also with its texture, which is a little bit of everything—crunchy, chewy, tender and moist. With its crusty base and creamy filling, you know the recipe is well worth the effort.

Serving Size: 12

Preparation & Cooking Time: 1 hour and 30 minutes

Ingredients:

- 2 tablespoons butter, melted
- 2 tablespoons sugar
- 1 ½ cups pecans, chopped

Cream Cheese Filling

- 16 oz. cream cheese
- 1 egg, beaten
- ¼ cup sugar
- ½ teaspoon vanilla extract

Pumpkin Filling

- 1 ¼ cups canned pumpkin puree
- 1 cup evaporated milk
- 2 eggs
- 1 teaspoon ground cinnamon
- ¼ teaspoon ground nutmeg
- ¼ teaspoon ground ginger
- ½ cup sugar
- Pinch salt
- ½ cup pecans, chopped

Instructions:

Mix the butter, sugar and pecans in a bowl.

Press the mixture into a pie pan.

Bake in the oven at 400 degrees F for 10 minutes.

In a bowl, mix the cream cheese, egg, sugar and vanilla extract.

Spread the mixture over the crust.

In another bowl, combine the canned pumpkin puree, evaporated milk, eggs, ground cinnamon, ground nutmeg, ground ginger, sugar and salt.

Spread the pumpkin puree mixture over the cream cheese filling.

Bake in the oven at 350 degrees F for 1 hour.

Let cool on a wire rack for 10 minutes.

Top with the pecans and serve.

10. Pumpkin Pecan Mini Pies

You are sure to get plenty of compliments when you serve these exquisite pumpkin pecan mini pies. For the final touches, cover with miniature chocolate chips or sprinkle with cinnamon sugar.

Serving Size: 20

Preparation & Cooking Time: 40 minutes

Ingredients:

- 3 ¼ cups all-purpose flour
- 2 teaspoons baking powder
- 2 teaspoons baking soda
- 1 teaspoon ground cloves
- 1 teaspoon ground nutmeg
- 1 ½ teaspoons ground cinnamon
- 1 ½ cups sugar
- ½ teaspoon salt
- 5 eggs
- ½ cup canola oil
- ½ cup water
- 15 oz. pumpkin puree
- 1 teaspoon vanilla extract

Filling

- 6 tablespoons all-purpose flour
- Pinch salt
- 1 cup almond milk
- 3 cups confectioners' sugar
- 1 ½ cups shortening
- 3 teaspoons vanilla extract

Toppings

- Ground cinnamon
- Mini chocolate chips
- Pecans, chopped and toasted

Instructions:

Preheat your oven to 350 degrees F.

Add the all-purpose flour, baking soda, baking powder, ground cloves, ground nutmeg, ground cinnamon, sugar and salt to a bowl.

In another bowl, beat together the eggs, canola oil, water, pumpkin puree and vanilla extract.

Add the egg mixture to the flour mixture.

Mix well.

Drop the mixture by spoonfuls into a baking pan.

Bake in the oven for 10 minutes.

Let cool on a wire rack.

Mix the all-purpose flour, salt, almond milk, confectioners' sugar, shortening and vanilla extract.

Beat until fluffy.

Spread the mixture on top of ½ of the pies.

Cover with the remaining pies.

Roll in ground cinnamon, mini chocolate chips or pecans.

11. Butter Pecan Cake

Your sweet tooth would be overly delighted with this great dessert—it is rich, creamy and easy to make too. Baking the unforgettable butter pecan cake will surely be the highlight of your week.

Serving Size: 12

Preparation & Cooking Time: 1 hour and 20 minutes

Ingredients:

- 3 tablespoons butter, melted
- 1 1/3 cups pecans, chopped
- 2/3 cup butter, softened
- 1 1/3 cups sugar
- 2 eggs
- 2 cups all-purpose flour
- ¼ teaspoon salt
- 1 ½ teaspoons baking powder
- 2/3 cup whole milk
- 1 ½ teaspoons vanilla extract

Frosting

- 3 cups confectioners' sugar
- 3 tablespoons butter, softened
- 3 tablespoons milk
- ¾ teaspoon vanilla extract

Instructions:

Pour the butter into a baking pan.

Add the pecans and toast at 350 degrees F for 10 minutes.

Beat together the sugar and butter until fluffy.

Stir in the eggs.

In a bowl, combine the all-purpose flour, salt and baking powder.

Add the flour mixture to the butter mixture.

Pour in the whole milk and vanilla extract.

Fold in ½ of the toasted pecans.

Mix well.

Pour the batter into a baking pan.

Bake in the oven at 350 degrees F for 30 minutes.

Let cool for 10 minutes.

Prepare the frosting by beating together the confectioners' sugar, butter, milk and vanilla extract.

Spread the frosting on all the sides of the cake.

12. Mixed Nut Bars

You will enjoy these crunchy pastries made with mixed nuts. Be sure to make a big batch of them to have enough for everyone.

Serving Size: 36

Preparation & Cooking Time: 30 minutes

Ingredients:

- 1 ½ cups all-purpose flour
- ¼ teaspoon salt
- ½ cup cold butter
- ¾ cup brown sugar
- 1 cup butterscotch chips
- 2 tablespoons cold butter
- ½ cup corn syrup
- 11 ½ oz. mixed nuts

Instructions:

Preheat your oven to 350 degrees F.

Add the all-purpose flour, salt and brown sugar to a bowl.

Stir in ½ cup of the cold butter.

Mix until crumbly.

Press 2 tablespoons of the crumbs into a baking pan.

Bake in the oven for 10 minutes.

Add the butterscotch chips and 2 tablespoons of the cold butter to a pan over medium heat.

Cook while stirring until melted.

Turn off the heat.

Stir in the corn syrup.

Pour the mixture over the crust.

Sprinkle with the mixed nuts on top.

Bake in the oven for 10 minutes.

Let cool on a wire rack.

Slice into bars.

13. Butter Pecan Cookie Bars

A pan of these cookie bars will surely go a long way in pleasing everyone's taste buds. The crunchy creamy treat makes a comforting autumn treat.

Serving Size: 2 dozen

Preparation & Cooking Time: 1 hour and 10 minutes

Ingredients:

- ½ cup butter, melted
- 2 cups brown sugar
- 1 tablespoon vanilla extract
- 2 eggs
- 2 cups all-purpose flour
- ½ teaspoon salt
- 1 cup pecans, chopped and divided

Icing

- 3 tablespoons butter
- ¼ cup dark brown sugar
- 1 tablespoon milk
- ½ cup confectioners' sugar

Instructions:

Preheat your oven to 350 degrees F.

Beat together the butter and brown sugar in a bowl.

Stir in the eggs and vanilla extract.

In another bowl, combine the all-purpose flour and salt.

Add the flour mixture to the butter mixture.

Stir in ½ of the pecans.

Pour the mixture into a baking pan.

Top with the remaining pecans.

Bake in the oven for 20 to 30 minutes.

Let cool on a wire rack.

Add the butter and dark brown sugar to a pan over low heat.

Cook while stirring for 30 seconds.

Pour in the milk and stir in the confectioners' sugar.

Drizzle the mixture over the bars.

Let cool for 10 minutes.

Slice into bars.

14. Pecan Pumpkin Dessert

These rich, buttery and chewy bars made with pecans and pumpkin are a delightful treat everyone will definitely enjoy. Rustle up a batch of them enough for everyone to enjoy.

Serving Size: 16

Preparation & Cooking Time: 1 hour and 15 minutes

Ingredients:

- 12 oz. evaporated milk
- 30 oz. pumpkin puree
- 3 eggs
- 1 cup sugar
- 1 teaspoon vanilla extract
- 15 oz. yellow cake mix
- 1 ½ cups pecans, chopped
- 1 cup butter, melted

Frosting

- 1 ½ cups confectioners' sugar
- 8 oz. cream cheese, softened
- 12 oz. whipped topping
- 1 teaspoon vanilla extract

Instructions:

Line your baking pan with parchment paper.

Beat together the evaporated milk, pumpkin puree, eggs, sugar and vanilla extract.

Pour the mixture into a baking pan.

Sprinkle the yellow cake mix and pecans on top.

Drizzle with the butter.

Bake in the oven at 350 degrees F for 1 hour or until golden.

Let cool on a wire rack.

Transfer the mixture to a serving platter.

In a bowl, beat together the confectioners' sugar, cream cheese, whipped topping and vanilla extract.

Frost the dessert bars with the icing.

15. Cinnamon Cookies

Once you have tried this incredible treat, you will find yourself craving it often. It is ideal for breakfast, for snack, or anytime you are in the mood for a sweet treat.

Serving Size: 7 dozen

Preparation & Cooking Time: 30 minutes

Ingredients:

- ½ cup shortening
- ½ cup butter, softened
- 1 cup white sugar
- ½ cup brown sugar
- 1 egg
- ½ teaspoon almond extract
- 1 teaspoon vanilla extract
- 2 ½ cups all-purpose flour
- 2 teaspoons baking soda
- 1 tablespoon ground cinnamon
- 2 teaspoons ground nutmeg
- 2 teaspoons cream of tartar
- 1 teaspoon lemon zest
- 2 teaspoons orange zest
- ½ teaspoon salt
- Additional white sugar

Instructions:

Cream the shortening, butter, sugars, egg and extracts.

In a bowl, combine the all-purpose flour, baking soda, ground cinnamon, ground nutmeg, cream of tartar, lemon zest, orange zest and salt.

Add the flour mixture to the butter mixture.

Form balls from the mixture.

Roll the balls into additional white sugar.

Place the balls in a baking pan.

Press to form cookies.

Bake in the oven at 350 degrees F for 15 minutes.

Let cool on a wire rack.

16. Cranberry Banana Bread

Here is a special treat that is easy to make even on regular busy days—bread made with cranberry, banana and pecans.

Serving Size: 12

Preparation & Cooking Time: 1 hour and 30 minutes

Ingredients:

- 2/3 cup sugar
- 1/3 cup shortening
- 1 cup ripe banana, mashed
- 1 teaspoon vanilla extract
- 2 eggs
- ¼ teaspoon baking soda
- 2 teaspoons baking powder
- 1 ¾ cups all-purpose flour
- ½ teaspoon salt
- ¾ cup pecans, chopped and divided
- 1 cup cranberry sauce
- ½ cup dried cranberries

Instructions:

Preheat your oven to 350 degrees F.

Beat together the sugar and shortening until crumbly.

Stir in the ripe banana, eggs and vanilla extract.

In another bowl, combine the all-purpose flour, baking soda, baking powder and salt.

Add the flour mixture into the sugar mixture.

Stir in ½ of the pecans.

Add the cranberry sauce and dried cranberries.

Pour the mixture into a loaf pan.

Top with the remaining pecans.

Bake in the oven for 50 minutes to 1 hour.

Let cool for 10 minutes before slicing and serving.

17. Pumpkin Muffins

If you love muffins, you will definitely enjoy these muffins, which are always a great idea for holidays and other special occasions.

Serving Size: 1 dozen

Preparation & Cooking Time: 40 minutes

Ingredients:

- ¼ cup brown sugar
- ½ cup white sugar
- ¼ cup butter, softened
- ½ cup buttermilk
- 2 eggs, lightly beaten
- 2/3 cup canned pumpkin puree
- 2 tablespoons molasses
- 1 teaspoon orange zest
- 2 cups all-purpose flour
- ¼ teaspoon salt
- ½ teaspoon baking powder
- 1 teaspoon baking soda
- 1 teaspoon pumpkin pie spice

Streusel Topping

- 1/3 cup all-purpose flour
- 2 tablespoons cold butter
- 3 tablespoons brown sugar

Instructions:

Preheat your oven to 375 degrees F.

Cream the sugars and butter in a bowl.

Stir in the buttermilk, eggs, canned pumpkin puree, molasses and orange zest.

In another bowl, combine the all-purpose flour, baking powder, baking soda, salt and pumpkin pie spice.

Add the flour mixture to the egg mixture.

Transfer the mixture to a muffin pan.

Prepare the topping by combining the all-purpose flour, cold butter and brown sugar.

Top the batter with the mixture.

Bake in the oven for 20 to 25 minutes.

Let cool on a wire rack for 5 minutes.

18. Oat & Coconut Cookies

These cookies are a wonderful way to cap any meal. You can also serve them as breakfast or snack.

Serving Size: 6 dozen

Preparation & Cooking Time: 40 minutes

Ingredients:

- ¾ cup pecans, chopped
- 1 cup coconut flakes
- ½ cup white sugar
- 1 ½ cups brown sugar
- 1 cup butter, softened
- 2 eggs
- 1 ½ teaspoons vanilla extract
- 1 teaspoon baking soda
- ½ teaspoon salt
- 2 cups all-purpose flour
- 2 cups chocolate chips
- 2 cups oats

Instructions:

Preheat your oven to 350 degrees F.

Spread the pecans and coconut flakes in a baking pan.

Bake in the oven for 6 minutes, stirring often.

Set aside and let cool.

Beat together the sugars and butter in a bowl.

Mix until fluffy.

Stir in the eggs and vanilla extract.

In another bowl, combine the all-purpose flour, salt and baking soda.

Add this to the butter mixture.

Stir in the toasted coconut flakes and pecans.

Fold in the chocolate chips and oats.

Drop by spoonfuls into a baking pan.

Bake in the oven at 350 degrees F for 12 to 15 minutes.

Let cool on a wire rack.

19. Maple Cinnamon Rolls

Mix up a batch of these amazing rolls sweetened with maple syrup and cinnamon and watch everyone's face light up.

Serving Size: 2 dozen

Preparation & Cooking Time: 40 minutes

Ingredients:

- 2/3 cup milk
- 1/3 cup maple syrup
- 1/3 cup butter, softened
- 1 egg
- ¾ teaspoon salt
- 3 cups bread flour
- ¼ oz. active dry yeast

Topping

- 2 tablespoons bread flour
- ½ cup brown sugar
- 6 tablespoons cold butter
- 4 teaspoons ground cinnamon

Icing

- 3 tablespoons butter, melted
- 1 cup confectioners' sugar
- 1 teaspoon milk
- 3 tablespoons maple syrup

Instructions:

Add the milk, maple syrup, butter, egg, salt, bread flour and active dry yeast to the bread making machine.

Choose the dough setting.

Once the cycle is complete, roll the dough into rectangles.

In a bowl, mix the bread flour, brown sugar, cold butter and ground cinnamon.

Mix until crumbly.

Top each of the dough rectangles with the mixture.

Roll up and pinch the seams.

Slice the roll into 12.

Add the rolls to a baking pan.

Cover the pan.

Let rise for 20 minutes.

Bake in the oven at 375 degrees F for 20 minutes.

Let cool on a wire rack for 5 minutes.

In another bowl, mix the butter, confectioners' sugar, milk and maple syrup.

Spread the icing over the rolls.

20. Double Peanut Butter Cake

You and your family will enjoy making this moist and fluffy double peanut butter cake and of course, devouring it afterwards.

Serving Size: 9

Preparation & Cooking Time: 50 minutes

Ingredients:

- ¼ cup butter, softened
- ½ cup creamy peanut butter
- 2 eggs
- ¾ cup sugar
- 1 ½ cups all-purpose flour
- ¼ teaspoon salt
- 2 teaspoons baking powder
- ¾ cup milk

Frosting

- 3 tablespoons butter, softened
- 1/3 cup chunky peanut butter
- ¼ cup milk
- 3 cups confectioners' sugar
- 1 ½ teaspoons vanilla extract
- Peanuts, chopped

Instructions:

Preheat your oven to 350 degrees F.

Beat together the butter, creamy peanut butter, eggs and sugar in a bowl for 4 to 5 minutes.

In a bowl, mix the all-purpose flour, salt and baking powder.

Add the flour mixture and milk to the butter mixture.

Mix well.

Pour the mixture into a baking pan.

Bake in the oven for 30 minutes.

Let cool on a wire rack.

Mix the butter, chunky peanut butter, milk, confectioners' sugar and vanilla extract.

Frost the cake with the mixture.

Top with peanuts.

21. Cranberry Zucchini Cake

Zucchini in cake? This is a surprisingly great idea that you would be happy to have discovered!

Serving Size: 16

Preparation & Cooking Time: 45 minutes

Ingredients:

- 20 oz. pineapple chunks
- 1 teaspoon baking soda
- 1 teaspoon baking powder
- 3 cups all-purpose flour
- 1 ¾ cups sugar
- 1 teaspoon salt
- 1 cup canola oil
- 3 eggs
- 2 teaspoons vanilla extract
- 1 cup cranberries, sliced in half
- 1 cup zucchini, shredded
- ½ cup walnuts, chopped
- Confectioners' sugar

Instructions:

Drain the pineapple chunks but reserve 1/3 cup of the pineapple juice.

Add the pineapple chunks and pineapple juice to the blender or food processor.

Process until smooth. Set aside.

In a bowl, mix the all-purpose flour, baking soda, baking powder, sugar and salt.

In another bowl, beat together the canola oil, eggs and vanilla extract.

Add the flour mixture to the egg mixture.

Fold in the pineapple mixture, cranberries, zucchini and walnuts.

Pour the mixture into a round baking pan.

Bake in the oven at 350 degrees F for 30 minutes.

Let cool for 10 minutes.

Dust the cake with confectioners' sugar.

22. Spice Cake

Here is an old-fashioned treat that has wonderful flavor and texture—a cake spiced with cinnamon, allspice, nutmeg and cloves.

Serving Size: 16

Preparation & Cooking Time: 1 hour and 10 minutes

Ingredients:

- ¾ cup butter, sliced into cubes
- 1 cup water
- 1 ½ cups sugar
- 1 cup raisins, chopped
- ½ teaspoon ground allspice
- 1 teaspoon ground cinnamon
- ¼ teaspoon ground nutmeg
- ¼ teaspoon ground cloves
- 4 eggs
- 2 cups all-purpose flour
- ½ teaspoon salt
- ¼ teaspoon baking soda
- 3 teaspoons baking powder
- ¾ cup pecans, chopped

Frosting

- ¼ cup butter
- 8 oz. cream cheese
- 1 teaspoon vanilla extract
- 4 cups confectioners' sugar
- Pinch salt

Topping

- Confectioners' sugar
- Bay leaves
- Cinnamon sticks
- Pecans, chopped

Instructions:

Add the butter, water, sugar, raisins and spices to a pan over medium heat.

Cook while stirring until the sugar is dissolved.

Turn off the heat. Let cool.

Beat the egg yolks and add to the spice mixture.

In a bowl, combine the all-purpose flour, baking powder, baking soda and salt.

Add this to the spice mixture.

Fold in the pecans.

Beat the egg whites until you see soft peaks forming.

Add this to the batter.

Pour the mixture into a round baking pan.

Bake in the oven at 325 degrees F for 35 to 40 minutes.

Let cool for 10 minutes.

Prepare the frosting by beating the butter, cream cheese, vanilla extract, confectioners' sugar and salt.

Frost all the sides of the cake.

Top with confectioners' sugar, bay leaves, cinnamon sticks and pecans.

23. Cinnamon Coffee Cake

Whenever you crave something sweet, here is an autumn inspired cake that you can actually make all year round—cinnamon coffee cake. Just make sure to mix carefully so that the cake will not turn out crumbly.

Serving Size: 20

Preparation & Cooking Time: 1 hour and 20 minutes

Ingredients:

- 2 ¾ cups sugar, divided
- 1 cup butter, softened
- 4 eggs
- 2 teaspoons vanilla extract
- 1 teaspoon salt
- 1 teaspoon baking soda
- 3 cups all-purpose flour
- 2 cups sour cream
- ½ cup walnuts, chopped
- 2 tablespoons ground cinnamon

Instructions:

Cream together 2 cups of the sugar and the butter until fluffy.

Stir in the eggs and vanilla extract.

In another bowl, combine the all-purpose flour, salt and baking soda.

Add this to the egg mixture alternately with the sour cream.

Pour 1/3 of the batter into a cake pan.

Mix the remaining sugar, walnuts and ground cinnamon.

Add 1/3 of the mixture on top of the batter.

Repeat the layers.

Bake in the oven at 350 degrees F for 1 hour.

Let cool for 15 minutes.

24. Maple Butter Twist

You will relish the excellent texture of this treat. Expect it to be a crowd pleaser each time you bring it out of the kitchen.

Serving Size: 32

Preparation & Cooking Time: 3 hours

Ingredients:

- 3 ½ cups all-purpose flour
- 3 tablespoons sugar
- ¼ oz. active dry yeast
- 1 ½ teaspoons salt
- ¾ cup milk
- ¼ cup butter
- 2 eggs

Filling

- 4 ½ teaspoons all-purpose flour
- 3 tablespoons butter, softened
- ¼ cup white sugar
- 1/3 cup brown sugar
- 3 tablespoons maple syrup
- ¾ teaspoon maple flavoring
- ¾ teaspoon ground cinnamon
- 1/3 cup walnuts, chopped

Glaze

- 3 teaspoons milk
- ¼ teaspoon maple flavoring
- ½ cup confectioners' sugar

Instructions:

Combine the all-purpose flour, sugar, active dry yeast and salt.

In a pan over medium heat, add the milk and butter.

Heat until the temperature reaches 120 degrees F.

Add the milk mixture to the flour mixture.

Mix well.

Stir in the eggs.

Knead the dough until smooth.

Transfer to a bowl.

Cover and let the dough rise for 1 hour and 10 minutes.

In another bowl, mix the all-purpose flour, butter, sugars, maple syrup, maple flavoring and ground cinnamon.

Punch down the dough and divide it into 2 pieces.

Roll each dough piece into a rectangle.

Top each dough rectangle with the filling and walnuts.

Roll it up.

Slice the roll in half lengthwise.

Twist the 2 parts together.

Transfer the twists to a round baking pan, coiling it to form a circle.

Tuck the ends and pinch the seals.

Cover and let rise for 45 minutes.

Bake in the oven at 350 degrees F for 30 minutes.

Let cool for 10 minutes.

In a small bowl, mix the milk, maple flavoring and confectioners' sugar.

Drizzle the mixture over the maple twists and serve.

25. Cookie Sticks

These are cookies but not round! When you make them for your family and friends, do not be surprised if they ask for another batch.

Serving Size: 3 dozen

Preparation & Cooking Time: 30 minutes

Ingredients:

- 1 egg
- ½ cup canola oil
- ½ cup brown sugar
- ½ cup white sugar
- 1 teaspoon vanilla extract
- 1 ½ cups all-purpose flour
- ½ teaspoon baking soda
- ½ teaspoon salt
- 1 cup chocolate chips
- ½ cup walnuts, chopped

Instructions:

Mix the egg, canola oil, sugars and vanilla extract in a bowl.

In another bowl, combine the all-purpose flour, salt and baking soda.

Add the flour mixture to the egg mixture.

Knead the dough and divide it into 2 pieces.

Shape each dough piece into a rectangle, and transfer to a baking pan.

Top with the walnuts and chocolate chips.

Press down onto the dough.

Bake in the oven at 375 degrees F for 7 minutes or until golden and crispy.

Let cool for 5 minutes before slicing into strips.

26. Butternut Squash Donuts

If you are craving donuts, this amazing treat will satisfy your sweet tooth. You will be happy that the recipe only takes minimal effort to prepare. There is a baking method alternative if you wish for a healthier version of it.

Serving Size: 2 dozen

Preparation & Cooking Time: 1 hour and 10 minutes

Ingredients:

- 1 cup butternut squash, cooked and mashed
- 2 tablespoons butter, softened
- 2 eggs
- ½ cup buttermilk
- 1 ¼ cups sugar
- 2 teaspoons vanilla extract
- 3 ½ cups all-purpose flour
- 1 teaspoon baking powder
- 1 ½ teaspoons baking soda
- 1 teaspoon cream of tartar
- 1 ¼ teaspoons ground nutmeg
- ¼ teaspoon ground ginger
- ¼ teaspoon ground cinnamon
- ½ teaspoon salt
- Oil
- Confectioners' sugar

Instructions:

In a bowl, combine the butternut squash, butter, eggs, buttermilk, sugar and vanilla extract.

In another bowl, mix the all-purpose flour, baking powder, baking soda, cream of tartar, ground nutmeg, ground ginger, ground cinnamon and salt.

Add the flour mixture to the squash mixture.

Mix well.

Refrigerate for 2 hours.

Roll the dough into a rectangle.

Cut with a donut cutter.

Pour oil into a pan over medium heat.

Heat the oil to 350 degrees F.

Fry the donuts for 1 to 2 minutes per side or until golden.

Or you can also bake in the oven at 350 degrees F for 20 minutes or until golden.

Dust with confectioners' sugar before serving.

27. Cranberry Chip Cookies

These cookies are so heavenly; you probably will not have words to describe how happy your sweet tooth is. The cranberries complement the chocolate chips and vanilla chips. Also, the pecans add extra crunch.

Serving Size: 6 dozen

Preparation & Cooking Time: 40 minutes

Ingredients:

- ¾ cup white sugar
- ¾ cup brown sugar
- ½ cup shortening
- 2 eggs
- ½ cup butter, softened
- 2 ¼ cups all-purpose flour
- 1 teaspoon vanilla extract
- ½ teaspoon salt
- 1 teaspoon baking soda
- 1 cup vanilla chips
- 1 cup chocolate chips
- 1 cup pecans, chopped
- 1 cup dried cranberries

Instructions:

Preheat your oven to 375 degrees F.

Cream together the butter, sugars and shortening until fluffy.

Stir in the eggs and vanilla extract.

In another bowl, mix the all-purpose flour, salt and baking soda.

Add the flour mixture to the butter mixture.

Fold in the vanilla chips, chocolate chips, pecans and dried cranberries.

Drop spoonfuls of the mixture onto a baking pan.

Bake in the oven for 10 minutes or until golden.

Let cool for 2 minutes before serving.

28. Chocolate Chip Pumpkin Bread

It is hard to get yourself away from this amazingly delicious chocolate chip pumpkin bread that is just the right amount of sweet and creamy.

Serving Size: 20

Preparation & Cooking Time: 1 hour and 20 minutes

Ingredients:

- 3 cups all-purpose flour
- 2 teaspoons ground cinnamon
- 1 teaspoon baking soda
- 1 teaspoon salt
- 4 eggs
- 1 ½ cups canola oil
- 2 cups sugar
- 2 cups canned pumpkin puree
- 1 ½ cups semisweet chocolate chips

Instructions:

Add the all-purpose flour, baking soda, ground cinnamon and salt to a bowl.

Stir in the eggs, canola oil, sugar and canned pumpkin puree.

Mix well.

Fold in the semisweet chocolate chips.

Pour the mixture into loaf pans.

Bake in the oven at 350 degrees F for 1 hour.

Let cool for 10 minutes before slicing and serving.

29. Toffee Pear Pudding

Here is a special dessert that easily becomes an autumn favorite—toffee and pear bread pudding.

Serving Size: 12

Preparation & Cooking Time: 1 hour and 30 minutes

Ingredients:

- ¼ cup butter, sliced into cubes
- 1 ¾ cups milk
- 1 cup butterscotch and caramel ice cream topping
- ½ teaspoon ground ginger
- 1 teaspoon ground cinnamon
- 2 eggs
- 4 cups day-old French bread, sliced into cubes
- 2 pears, peeled and sliced

Topping

- ½ cup all-purpose flour
- ½ cup brown sugar
- 1/3 cup cold butter
- 1/3 cup English toffee bits

Instructions:

Preheat your oven to 350 degrees F.

Add the butter, milk, butterscotch and caramel ice cream topping, ground ginger and ground cinnamon to a pan over medium heat.

Cook while stirring until the butter has melted.

Turn off the heat.

Beat the eggs in a bowl.

Add the milk mixture.

Mix well.

Stir in the day-old French bread and pears.

Let sit for 10 minutes.

Transfer the mixture to a baking pan.

In another bowl, combine the all-purpose flour, brown sugar, cold butter and English toffee bits.

Layer the mixture in the baking pan.

Bake in the oven for 20 minutes.

Let sit for 10 minutes before serving.

30. Cranberry Drop Cookies

Soft cranberry drop cookies drizzled with frosting make a cozy autumn treat that you and your family will enjoy.

Serving Size: 5 dozen

Preparation & Cooking Time: 40 minutes

Ingredients:

- ½ cup butter, softened
- 1 egg
- 1 cup white sugar
- ¾ cup brown sugar
- ¼ cup milk
- 2 tablespoons orange juice
- 3 cups all-purpose flour
- ½ teaspoon salt
- 1 teaspoon baking powder
- ¼ teaspoon baking soda
- 1 cup walnuts, chopped
- 2 ½ cups cranberries, chopped

Frosting

- 1/3 cup butter
- 2 cups confectioners' sugar
- 1 ½ teaspoons vanilla extract
- 3 tablespoons hot water

Instructions:

Cream the butter, egg and sugars in a bowl.

Stir in the milk and orange juice.

In another bowl, combine the all-purpose flour, baking powder, baking soda and salt.

Add the flour mixture to the egg mixture.

Fold in the walnuts and cranberries.

Drop by spoonfuls onto a baking pan.

Bake in the oven at 350 degrees F for 15 minutes.

Let cool on a wire rack.

For the frosting, add the butter to a pan over low heat.

Cook for 5 minutes.

Let cool for 2 minutes.

Add the confectioners' sugar, vanilla extract and hot water.

Frost the cookies before serving.

31. Sweet Potato Mini Cakes

Prepare these incredible mini cakes when you have friends coming over and you want to serve them something they will never forget. They are creamy, tender and rich—a satisfying dessert that is also easy to make.

Serving Size: 24

Preparation & Cooking Time: 1 hour and 20 minutes

Ingredients:

- 2 cups all-purpose flour
- 1 cup brown sugar
- 1 cup white sugar
- 1 teaspoon baking powder
- 1 teaspoon baking soda
- 1 teaspoon pumpkin pie spice
- 1 teaspoon ground cinnamon
- 1 teaspoon salt
- 1 ¼ cups canola oil
- 4 eggs
- 3 cups sweet potatoes, shredded
- 8 oz. pineapple chunks
- 1 teaspoon rum extract
- 1 cup walnuts, chopped
- 1 cup raisins

Frosting

- 8 oz. cream cheese
- 1 cup butter
- 5 cups confectioners' sugar
- 4 teaspoons brown sugar
- ½ teaspoon rum extract
- 1 teaspoon vanilla extract
- 1 ½ cups walnuts, crushed

Instructions:

In a bowl, combine the all-purpose flour, brown sugar, white sugar, baking powder, baking soda, pumpkin pie spice, ground cinnamon and salt.

Stir in the canola oil, egg, sweet potatoes, pineapple chunks, rum extract, walnuts and raisins.

Pour the mixture into muffin cups.

Bake in the oven at 350 degrees F for 30 minutes.

Let cool for 10 minutes.

In another bowl, beat together the butter and cream cheese until light and fluffy.

Stir in the confectioners' sugar, brown sugar, rum extract and vanilla extract.

Frost all the sides of the cake.

Roll in the walnuts.

32. Applesauce Spiced Cupcakes

Whenever you are craving sweet treats but do not want to exert too much effort in preparation, this recipe works wonders each time.

Serving Size: 1 dozen

Preparation & Cooking Time: 45 minutes

Ingredients:

- 2 eggs
- 1/3 cup butter, softened
- ¾ cup sugar
- 1 teaspoon vanilla extract
- ½ teaspoon baking soda
- 1 teaspoon baking powder
- 1 1/3 cups all-purpose flour
- 1/8 teaspoon ground cloves
- ½ teaspoon ground nutmeg
- 1 teaspoon ground cinnamon
- ½ teaspoon salt
- ¾ cup applesauce
- 1 cup cream cheese frosting

Instructions:

Whisk together the eggs, butter, sugar and vanilla extract in a bowl.

In another bowl, mix the all-purpose flour, baking powder, baking soda, ground cloves, ground nutmeg, ground cinnamon and salt.

Add the flour mixture to the egg mixture.

Stir in the applesauce.

Pour the mixture into muffin cups.

Bake in the oven at 350 degrees F for 30 minutes.

Let cool for 10 minutes before serving.

Frost the top with the cream cheese frosting.

33. Mexican Chocolate Pastries

This recipe captures the exquisite combination of chocolate, cinnamon and walnut. Make the most out of autumn with the incredible pastries.

Serving Size: 2 ½ dozen

Preparation & Cooking Time: 1 hour and 30 minutes

Ingredients:

- 2 ¾ cups all-purpose flour
- 1 cup cocoa powder
- 1 ½ teaspoons baking soda
- 2 cups sugar
- 2 teaspoons chocolate cinnamon cane sugar
- 5 eggs
- 2 teaspoons vanilla extract
- 1 cup chocolate chips
- 6 oz. cherries, sliced in half
- 1 ½ cups walnuts, chopped and toasted

Instructions:

Preheat your oven to 325 degrees F.

In a bowl, mix the all-purpose flour, cocoa powder, baking soda, sugar and chocolate cinnamon cane sugar.

In another bowl, combine the eggs and vanilla extract.

Add the egg mixture to the flour mixture.

Fold in the chocolate chips, walnuts and cherries.

Knead until the dough is formed.

Divide the dough into 3 portions.

Shape into a rectangle.

Bake in the oven for 30 minutes.

Let cool on a wire rack for 10 minutes.

Slice the cake into strips.

Bake in the oven at 300 degrees F for 10 minutes per side.

Let cool before serving.

34. Gingerbread Cake with Caramel

Here is a timeless recipe that is made even better with whipped cream and caramel sauce. It only takes 1 hour or so to get the wonderful dessert done.

Serving Size: 9

Preparation & Cooking Time: 1 hour and 15 minutes

Ingredients:

- 1 egg
- 9 tablespoons butter, softened
- 1/3 cup sugar
- 1 cup molasses
- 2 ¼ cups all-purpose flour
- 1 teaspoon baking soda
- 1 teaspoon ground cinnamon
- 1 teaspoon ground ginger
- ¼ teaspoon salt
- ¾ cup water

Caramel Sauce

- 1 tablespoon cornstarch
- 1 cup brown sugar
- 1 cup cold water
- 1 teaspoon vanilla extract
- ¼ cup butter, melted
- Whipped cream

Instructions:

Beat together the egg, butter, sugar and molasses.

Stir in the all-purpose flour, baking soda, ground cinnamon, ground ginger, salt and water.

Transfer the mixture to a baking pan.

Bake in the oven at 325 degrees F for 40 minutes.

In a pan over medium heat, mix the cornstarch, brown sugar and cold water.

Bring to a boil.

Reduce the heat and simmer for 2 minutes or until the sauce has thickened.

Turn off the heat.

Stir in the vanilla extract and butter.

Slice and top with the whipped cream and caramel sauce.

35. Spiced Pumpkin Bars

You will love the bold but delicious combination of pumpkin and spices. This is an elegant autumn dessert that only takes 30 minutes to prepare.

Serving Size: 32

Preparation & Cooking Time: 30 minutes

Ingredients:

- 2 cups all-purpose flour
- 1 tablespoon baking powder
- 1 teaspoon baking soda
- 1 ½ cups sugar
- ¼ teaspoon ground cloves
- ¼ teaspoon ground nutmeg
- ½ teaspoon ground ginger
- 2 teaspoons ground cinnamon
- ½ teaspoon salt
- 4 eggs
- 1 cup unsweetened applesauce
- 15 oz. pumpkin puree
- Confectioners' sugar

Instructions:

Mix the all-purpose flour, baking soda, baking powder, sugar, ground cinnamon, ground cloves, ground ginger, ground nutmeg and salt in a bowl.

Stir in the eggs, unsweetened applesauce and pumpkin puree.

Spread the mixture into a baking pan.

Bake in the oven at 350 degrees F for 20 minutes.

Let cool on a wire rack.

Slice and then dust with confectioners' sugar.

36. Caramel Apple Tart

An apple a day helps you prepare incredible desserts! Here is an apple dessert that only takes a few minutes to prepare. You will love the crunchy crust and the rich caramel topping.

Serving Size: 4

Preparation & Cooking Time: 45 minutes

Ingredients:

- 2/3 cup all-purpose flour
- 1/8 teaspoon salt
- 1 tablespoon sugar
- ¼ cup cold butter, sliced into cubes
- 1/8 teaspoon vanilla extract
- 6 ½ teaspoons cold water

Filling

- 1 tablespoon all-purpose flour
- 1 ½ cups apple, peeled and chopped
- 3 tablespoons sugar

Topping

- ¼ teaspoon ground cinnamon
- 1 teaspoon sugar
- 1 egg
- 1 tablespoon water
- 2 tablespoons caramel ice cream topping

Instructions:

Mix the all-purpose flour, salt and sugar in a bowl.

Stir in the cold butter.

Mix until the texture is crumbly.

Pour in the vanilla extract and cold water.

Mix until the dough is formed.

Cover the bowl.

Refrigerate for 30 minutes.

Preheat your oven to 400 degrees F.

Roll the dough into a circle.

Transfer the dough to a pie pan.

Combine the all-purpose flour, apple and sugar.

Top the crust with the filling.

Fold the edges over the filling but leave the middle part uncovered.

Mix the ground cinnamon and sugar.

Sprinkle the mixture on top of the filling.

Mix the egg and water.

Brush the top with the egg wash.

Bake in the oven for 30 minutes or until golden and crispy.

Drizzle the top with the caramel ice cream topping before serving.

Serve immediately.

37. Coffee Cookies

Any coffee lover will enjoy these easy-to-make cookies made with instant coffee granules. They will last 3 to 5 days at room temperature and up to 6 months frozen.

Serving Size: 5 dozen

Preparation & Cooking Time: 35 minutes

Ingredients:

- ¾ cup vegetable oil
- 1 cup white sugar
- 2 tablespoons hot water
- 1/3 cup instant coffee granules
- 2 eggs
- 2 ½ cups all-purpose flour
- ¾ teaspoon salt
- 1 ½ teaspoons baking powder
- Additional white sugar

Instructions:

Preheat your oven to 400 degrees F.

Mix the vegetable oil and white sugar in a bowl.

Pour the hot water into a cup.

Add the instant coffee granules.

Stir until dissolved.

Add the coffee mixture to the sugar mixture.

Stir in the eggs.

In another bowl, mix the all-purpose flour, salt and baking powder.

Add this to the coffee mixture.

Roll the mixture into balls.

Flatten and sprinkle with additional white sugar.

Place the cookies in a baking pan.

Bake in the oven for 10 minutes.

Let cool on a wire rack.

38. Dutch Apple Cake

Warm up on a cold night with this cake made with apple, cinnamon, butter and vanilla. The recipe takes minimal effort but tastes grand.

Serving Size: 12

Preparation & Cooking Time: 2 hours and 10 minutes

Ingredients:

- 3 apples, peeled and chopped
- 1 teaspoon ground cinnamon
- 3 tablespoons white sugar
- 2/3 cup butter, softened
- 1 cup white sugar
- 4 eggs
- 1 teaspoon vanilla extract
- 2 cups all-purpose flour
- 1/8 teaspoon salt

Instructions:

Toss the apples in the ground cinnamon and 3 tablespoons of the white sugar.

Let sit for 1 hour.

In a bowl, mix the butter and 1 cup of the white sugar.

Mix until fluffy.

Stir in the eggs and vanilla extract.

In another bowl, combine the all-purpose flour and salt.

Add the flour mixture to the egg mixture.

Mix until smooth.

Transfer the mixture to a loaf pan.

Press the mixed apples into the batter.

Bake the cake in the oven at 300 degrees F for 1 hour and 30 minutes.

Let cool before slicing and serving.

39. Cashew Cookies

These cookies are so good and so easy to make that you would find them frequently in your potluck parties and get-togethers.

Serving Size: 5 dozen

Preparation & Cooking Time: 40 minutes

Ingredients:

- ½ cup butter, softened
- 1 cup brown sugar
- 1 egg
- ¾ teaspoon baking soda
- ¾ teaspoon baking powder
- ½ teaspoon vanilla extract
- ¼ teaspoon salt
- 1/3 cup sour cream
- 2 cups all-purpose flour
- 1 ¾ cups cashews, chopped

Frosting

- ½ cup butter, sliced into cubes
- 3 tablespoons half and half cream
- 2 cups confectioners' sugar
- ¼ teaspoon vanilla extract
- 1 cup cashews, sliced in half

Instructions:

Preheat your oven to 375 degrees F.

Add the butter and brown sugar in a bowl.

Cream together until fluffy.

Stir in the egg and vanilla extract.

In a bowl, mix the all-purpose flour, baking powder, baking soda and salt.

Add the flour mixture and sour cream to the egg mixture.

Fold in the cashews.

Drop by spoonfuls onto a baking pan.

Bake in the oven for 10 minutes.

Let cool on a wire rack.

Add the butter to a pan over medium heat.

Let the butter brown a little.

Turn off the heat.

Add the browned butter to a bowl.

Stir in the half and half cream, confectioners' sugar and vanilla extract.

Frost the cookies with the icing and press the cashews on top.

40. Pumpkin Cheesecake Dessert

You cannot help but be merry with this amazing dessert that is a combination of pumpkin pie and cheesecake. Serve with glaze and whipped cream on top.

Serving Size: 24

Preparation & Cooking Time: 1 hour and 15 minutes

Ingredients:

- ¼ cup butter, melted
- 1 ½ cups gingersnap cookies, crushed
- 1 cup sugar
- 40 oz. cream cheese
- 1 teaspoon ground cinnamon
- 15 oz. pureed pumpkin
- 1 teaspoon vanilla extract
- 5 eggs, beaten
- Ground nutmeg
- Sweetened whipped cream
- Maple syrup

Instructions:

Mix the butter and gingersnap cookies.

Press the mixture into a pie pan. Set aside.

Whisk together the sugar and cream cheese until smooth.

Stir in the ground cinnamon, pureed pumpkin and vanilla extract.

Add the eggs.

Beat the mixture until fully combined.

Pour the mixture on top of the crust.

Top with ground nutmeg.

Bake in the oven at 350 degrees F for 45 minutes.

Let cool on a wire rack.

Slice into squares.

Serve with sweetened whipped cream and maple syrup.

41. Butter Brownies

With its rich chocolate flavor, this dessert certainly would be hard to resist. Expect to get rave reviews when you serve the brownies to your family or friends.

Serving Size: 4 dozen

Preparation & Cooking Time: 50 minutes

Ingredients:

- 1 ½ cups butter, divided
- ¾ cup cocoa powder, divided
- 4 eggs
- 1 teaspoon vanilla extract
- 2 cups sugar
- 1 ½ cups all-purpose flour
- ½ teaspoon salt
- 16 oz. peanut butter
- 1/3 cup milk
- 10 marshmallows
- 2 cups confectioners' sugar

Instructions:

Preheat your oven to 350 degrees F.

Add 1 cup of the butter to a pan over medium heat.

Once melted, add ½ cup of the cocoa powder.

Mix until smooth.

Turn off the heat.

In a bowl, whisk together the eggs, vanilla extract and sugar.

In another bowl, mix the all-purpose flour and salt.

Add the flour mixture to the egg mixture.

Stir in the cocoa mixture.

Transfer the mixture to a baking pan.

Bake in the oven for 20 minutes.

Let cool on a wire rack.

Warm the peanut butter in the microwave for 30 seconds.

Spread the peanut butter on top of the brownies.

Refrigerate for 45 minutes.

In a pan over medium low heat, add the milk, marshmallows, remaining butter and remaining cocoa powder.

Cook while stirring until smooth.

Turn off the heat.

Stir in the confectioners' sugar.

Spread the mixture on top of the peanut butter layer.

Refrigerate for 30 minutes.

Slice into squares.

42. Pumpkin Cookies

A real crowd pleaser, these cookies with creamy frosting are everything you like in cookies—gooey, crunchy, sweet, flavorful and best of all, easy to make.

Serving Size: 3 dozen

Preparation & Cooking Time: 1 hour and 10 minutes

Ingredients:

- 1 cup butter, softened
- ½ cup brown sugar
- ½ cup white sugar
- 1 egg
- 1 cup all-purpose flour
- 1 cup whole wheat flour
- 1 cup canned pumpkin puree
- ½ teaspoon baking soda
- 1 teaspoon baking powder
- 1 teaspoon ground ginger
- 1 ½ teaspoons ground cinnamon
- ¼ teaspoon ground cloves
- ½ teaspoon ground nutmeg
- ½ teaspoon salt
- 1 cup granola (raisins removed)
- 1 cup dried cranberries
- 1 cup white chocolate chips
- 1 cup walnuts, chopped

Icing

- 3 tablespoons milk
- 2 cups confectioners' sugar
- ¼ cup butter

Instructions:

Beat together the butter, white sugar and brown sugar in a bowl until fluffy.

Stir in the egg and canned pumpkin puree.

In a bowl, mix the whole wheat flour, all-purpose flour, baking soda, baking powder, ground ginger, ground cinnamon, ground cloves, ground nutmeg and salt.

Add the flour mixture to the egg mixture.

Fold in the granola, dried cranberries, white chocolate chips and walnuts.

Drop spoonfuls of the mixture onto a baking sheet.

Bake in the oven at 350 degrees F for 15 minutes.

Let cool on a wire rack.

In a bowl, combine the milk, confectioners' sugar and butter.

Spread the mixture on top of the cookies.

43. Cranberry Chip Cookies

These cookies are anything but boring. You will love the combination of chocolate chips, dried cranberries, pecans and English toffee bits.

Serving Size: 6 dozen

Preparation & Cooking Time: 30 minutes

Ingredients:

- 1 cup sugar
- 1 cup butter, softened
- 1 teaspoon vanilla extract
- 2 eggs
- 2 ¼ cups all-purpose flour
- ¼ teaspoon salt
- ½ teaspoon baking powder
- ½ cup English toffee bits
- ¾ cup pecans, chopped
- 1 ½ cups chocolate chips
- 1 ½ cups dried cranberries

Instructions:

Beat together the sugar and butter in a bowl.

Stir in the vanilla extract and eggs.

In another bowl, combine the all-purpose flour, salt and baking powder.

Add the flour mixture to the butter mixture.

Fold in the English toffee bits, pecans, chocolate chips and dried cranberries.

Drop spoonfuls of the mixture onto a baking pan.

Bake in the oven at 350 degrees F for 15 minutes.

Let cool on a wire rack before serving.

44. Baked Apple Dumplings

Do not wait until there is a special occasion to make these incredible baked apple dumplings. They are easy enough to make at any time.

Serving Size: 8

Preparation & Cooking Time: 50 minutes

Ingredients:

- 16 oz. refrigerated crescent rolls
- 2 apples, peeled and sliced into wedges
- 1/3 cup butter, softened
- ½ teaspoon ground cinnamon
- 1 cup sugar
- Vanilla ice cream

Instructions:

Preheat your oven to 350 degrees F.

Separate the refrigerated crescent rolls into triangles.

Top the triangles with the apples.

Wrap and place in a baking pan.

In a bowl, mix the butter, ground cinnamon and sugar.

Brush the mixture on top of the dumplings.

Bake in the oven for 40 minutes.

Serve with vanilla ice cream.

45. Chocolate Maple Bars

Need a simple but impressive dessert that you can make with no hassle? Try these bars topped with creamy chocolate and mini marshmallows.

Serving Size: 3 dozen

Preparation & Cooking Time: 45 minutes

Ingredients:

- ½ cup shortening
- ½ cup sugar
- ¾ cup maple syrup
- 3 eggs
- 1 teaspoon vanilla extract
- 3 tablespoons milk
- 1 ¼ cups all-purpose flour
- ¼ teaspoon salt
- ¼ teaspoon baking powder
- ½ cup pecans, chopped
- 1 ½ oz. chocolate, melted
- ½ cup sweetened coconut flakes

Frosting

- ¼ cup butter, softened
- 1 cup confectioners' sugar
- ½ cup baking cocoa
- ½ cup maple syrup
- 1 cup mini marshmallows

Instructions:

Preheat your oven to 350 degrees F.

Cream together the shortening, sugar and maple syrup for 5 minutes or until fluffy.

Stir in the eggs, vanilla extract and milk.

In another bowl, combine the all-purpose flour, salt and baking powder.

Add the flour mixture to the egg mixture.

Divide the mixture into 2 bowls.

Add the pecans and chocolate to the first bowl.

Fold the sweetened coconut flakes to the second bowl.

Spread the chocolate mixture into a baking pan.

Spread the coconut flake mixture on top.

Bake in the oven for 25 minutes.

Let cool on a wire rack.

Beat the butter until smooth.

Add the baking cocoa and confectioners' sugar.

Stir in the maple syrup and add the mini marshmallows.

Frost the bars.

46. Cranberry Muffins

These muffins are truly delightful. Every bite brings pleasure and satiates your sweet cravings. They are pure autumn bliss!

Serving Size: 2 dozen

Preparation & Cooking Time: 30 minutes

Ingredients:

- 2 ¼ cups all-purpose flour
- ½ teaspoon salt
- 1 teaspoon pumpkin pie spice
- 1 teaspoon baking soda
- ½ cup canola oil
- 2 eggs
- 1 cup canned pumpkin puree
- 2 cups sugar
- 1 cup cranberries, chopped

Instructions:

Preheat your oven to 400 degrees F.

Combine the pumpkin pie spice, all-purpose flour, baking soda and salt.

In another bowl, mix the canola oil, eggs, canned pumpkin puree and sugar.

Add the flour mixture to the egg mixture.

Fold in the cranberries.

Pour the mixture into muffin cups.

Bake in the oven for 20 minutes.

Let cool for 5 minutes before serving.

47. Apple & Pear Coffee Cake

Coffee balances the flavor of apple and pear in this delicious cake that takes only 1 hour and 10 minutes to make.

Serving Size: 12

Preparation & Cooking Time: 1 hour and 10 minutes

Ingredients:

- 1 cup sugar
- ½ cup butter, softened
- 2 eggs
- 1 teaspoon vanilla extract
- 1 teaspoon baking powder
- 1 teaspoon baking soda
- 2 cups all-purpose flour
- ½ teaspoon salt
- 1 cup sour cream
- 1 pear, peeled and chopped
- 1 apple, peeled and chopped
- 1 cup brown sugar
- 2 tablespoons butter
- 1 teaspoon ground cinnamon
- ½ cup walnuts, chopped

Instructions:

Preheat your oven to 350 degrees F.

Mix the sugar and butter in a bowl.

Stir in the eggs and vanilla extract.

In another bowl, combine the all-purpose flour, baking soda, baking powder and salt.

Add the flour mixture to the butter mixture.

Stir in the sour cream.

Fold in the pear and apple.

Spread the mixture into a baking pan.

Prepare the topping by mixing the brown sugar, butter, ground cinnamon and walnuts.

Spread this on top of the batter.

Bake in the oven for 30 minutes.

Let cool on a wire rack before serving.

48. Sweet Potato Crisp

Here is a hassle-free dessert that you can prepare even on busy nights—sweet potato crisp with fig and pear. Serve with vanilla ice cream on the side.

Serving Size: 8

Preparation & Cooking Time: 50 minutes

Ingredients:

- 30 oz. sweet potatoes, peeled and chopped
- 2 pears, peeled and chopped
- 8 oz. dried figs, sliced
- ¼ cup maple syrup
- 1 teaspoon lemon juice
- ½ teaspoon ground allspice
- 1 cup pecans, chopped
- 1 cup rolled oats
- 1/3 cup all-purpose flour
- ¼ cup brown sugar
- ¼ teaspoon ground allspice
- 1 teaspoon ground cinnamon
- 1/3 cup canola oil
- 1/8 teaspoon salt
- 1 tablespoon maple syrup
- Vanilla ice cream

Instructions:

Preheat your oven to 350 degrees F.

In a bowl, mix all the ingredients except vanilla ice cream.

Transfer the mixture to a baking pan.

Bake in the oven for 40 minutes.

Serve with vanilla ice cream.

49. Pumpkin Chip Cookies

Do not be surprised if these cookies disappear right before your eyes. They are truly delectable.

Serving Size: 10 dozen

Preparation & Cooking Time: 20 minutes

Ingredients:

- 1 cup white sugar
- 2 cups brown sugar
- 1 ½ cups butter, softened
- 1 egg
- 1 teaspoon vanilla extract
- 15 oz. pumpkin puree
- 4 cups all-purpose flour
- 1 teaspoon salt
- 2 teaspoons ground cinnamon
- 2 teaspoons baking soda
- 2 cups chocolate chips
- 2 cups instant oats

Instructions:

Preheat your oven to 350 degrees F.

Beat together the sugars and butter until fluffy.

Stir in the egg, pumpkin puree and vanilla extract in a bowl.

In another bowl, combine the all-purpose flour, ground cinnamon, baking soda and salt.

Add the flour mixture to the butter mixture.

Stir in the chocolate chips and instant oats.

Drop by spoonfuls into a baking pan.

Bake in the oven for 10 minutes.

Let cool on a wire rack before serving.

50. Gingerbread Scones

Bake these comforting gingerbread scones for snack or dessert when the fall season rolls in.

Serving Size: 1 dozen

Preparation & Cooking Time: 35 minutes

Ingredients:

- 2 cups all-purpose flour
- 3 tablespoons brown sugar
- ½ teaspoon baking soda
- 2 teaspoons baking powder
- 1 teaspoon ground ginger
- ½ teaspoon ground cinnamon
- ½ teaspoon salt
- ¼ cup cold butter, sliced into cubes
- ¼ cup milk
- 1/3 cup molasses
- 1 egg yolk
- 1 egg white
- Coarse sugar

Instructions:

Preheat your oven to 400 degrees F.

In a bowl, mix the all-purpose flour, brown sugar, baking soda, baking powder, ground ginger, ground cinnamon and salt.

Stir in the cold butter until the mixture is crumbly.

In another bowl, beat together the milk, molasses and egg yolk.

Add this to the flour mixture.

Knead the dough.

Form the dough into a circle.

Slice into wedges.

Place the wedges in a baking pan.

Beat the egg white until frothy.

Brush the top of the scones with the egg white.

Sprinkle with coarse sugar.

Bake in the oven for 15 minutes.

Conclusion

That is it!

You have enough autumn baking recipes to last the whole season!

For sure, you are going to enjoy making these recipes, and of course, eating the treats afterwards.

These are sure to delight your family and friends as well.

Enjoy!

Biography

Cooking is second nature to Olivia. This is not a surprise as she comes from a family of chefs. Cooking runs in the Rana family, and it is no wonder that Olivia didn't bother trying to find her root in life.

It was as if her path in life had been preordained for her. She knew that all she wanted to do in life was to be a food expert.

So, after college, she started a small restaurant in her town and launched a culinary school by the side.

Both businesses are doing well, and Olivia has expanded the businesses to a very admirable length.

❁❁❁❁❁❁❁❁❁❁❁❁❁❁❁

Afterword

Readers like you are the reason I get up in the morning. I am delighted that you decided to download and read my Books.

I can't thank you enough for choosing healthy living via your choice to engage in healthy and creative cooking. It means a lot to me because I poured my heart and passion into every page of this cookbook. And this is why I hope that you'd get absolute fulfillment from reading and exploring cooking with this recipe book.

I know that there are lots of similar culinary content like this everywhere, but it gives me joy that you chose mine. Hence, I'd appreciate it if you could help with your thoughts about this book. Feedback from customers helps me do better, so I don't mind getting a few from you.

You can do that by leaving a review on Amazon.com.

Thanks!

Olivia Rana

Printed in Great Britain
by Amazon